How to Create Your Own ERC-20 Token and Launch an ICO

Table of Contents:

Chapter 5: Deploying to the Ropsten Testnet
-Choosing a Testnet
-Obtaining Test Ether
-Configuring Truffle for Deployment
-Verifying on Etherscan
-Transacting on Ropsten

Chapter 6: Planning Your Token Sale
-Evaluating Sale Models
-Setting Pricing and Valuation
-Establishing Caps and Constraints
-Creating a Distribution Split
-Marketing and Exchange Listing Strategy

Chapter 7: Launching Your Token Generation Event
-Building a Dedicated Website
-Integrating a Sale Portal
-Airdropping Tokens
-Executing Your Marketing Plan
-Opening and Closing the Sale

Chapter 8: Distributing Tokens and Listing
-Transferring Tokens to Purchasers
-Getting Listed on Exchanges
-Promoting Liquidity and Trading
-Launching Staking and Governance -Continuing Development

A Deep Dive: Chapters 9-17

Chapter 9: Advanced Tokenomics and Distribution Strategies

Chapter 10: ERC-20 Token Types and Use Cases

Chapter 11: Alternative Blockchains Supporting Ethereum Smart Contracts

Chapter 12: Leveraging Decentralized Exchanges

Chapter 13: Securing Tokens - Web3 Wallets and Best Practices

Step 1 - Install Development Tools

You will need:

- Node.js to run JavaScript-based apps outside a browser
- npm for managing Node.js packages
- Solidity compiler to convert Solidity code into bytecode
- Ganache to set up a local Ethereum test blockchain
- Metamask Ethereum wallet extension for Chrome
- Truffle suite for smart contract development

Step 2 - Design the Token

Decide on the token details:

- Token name & symbol
- Total supply
- Decimal places
- Minting process
- Vision for project & token distribution

Develop a full prospectus to describe the token's value proposition.

Step 3 - Write the Smart Contract

Use Solidity to code the core smart contract containing:
- Token name and symbol
- Total supply and decimal precision
- Balances mapping to store account balances
- Transfer event for transfers
- Transfer function to transfer tokens
- Approve and transferFrom functions for allowances
- Owner address variable
- Constructor code to mint initial supply to the owner

Use OpenZeppelin's libraries to simplify contract logic.

Step 4 - Test the Smart Contract

In Truffle, write Javascript-based tests for key functions:
- Deploying the contract
- Transferring tokens
- Approving and transferring from allowances
- Querying balances and allowances

Understand Ethereum gas costs and optimize code to lower costs.

Step 5 - Deploy to Testnet

Use Ganache to launch a local test blockchain. Deploy the contract and run tests.
Obtain ether from a Ropsten faucet. Deploy to the Ropsten testnet and run tests again.
Verify the deployment using Etherscan's Ropsten Explorer.

Step 6 - Plan Token Sale

Decide on a fund raising model:
- Crowdsale
- Dutch auction
- Interactive coin offering

Determine pricing model, fundraising caps, and distribution proportions.

Draft legal documents for token sale including disclaimers.

Step 7 - Launch Token Sale

Set up website with token sale portal and ability to purchase tokens using ETH.
Market token sale through various channels like crypto forums.
Airdrop tokens to early supporters to generate initial interest.

Step 8 - Distribute Tokens

Once sale completes, distribute tokens to contributors' Ethereum wallet addresses.
List the token on exchanges like Uniswap and provide trading pairs like WBTC-USDC.
Add tokens to holder's wallets and publish trading data to CoinMarketCap, CoinGecko etc.
Building an engaged community and providing token utility beyond speculation are key success factors as well. But this guide covers the technical foundations

Step by Step Guide

Step 1 - Install Development Tools

To code and deploy an ERC-20 token, you first need to set up some essential programming tools locally on your computer:

Node.js

Node.js is an open-source JavaScript runtime environment that allows developers to run JavaScript code outside of a web browser.
Here's how to install it:
1. Go to https://nodejs.org/en/ and download the LTS version of Node.js for your operating system.
2. Run the installer .msi or .pkg file and follow the installation prompts.
3. Restart your computer to complete the installation.

4. To confirm it was installed properly, open your terminal and type `node --version`. This should print the version number.

Node.js contains the key components needed to execute JavaScript code and interact with tooling like npm and Truffle.

npm

npm stands for Node Package Manager. It is the default package manager included with Node.js.

npm allows you to install and manage open-source Node.js packages from the https://www.npmjs.com/ repository.

To verify npm is installed, run `npm --version` in your terminal.

We will use npm to install packages like Truffle later.

Solidity Compiler

Solidity is the main programming language used to write smart contracts on Ethereum. The Solidity compiler converts Solidity source code into bytecode that can execute on the Ethereum Virtual Machine (EVM).

Here's how to install it:

1. In your terminal, run: `npm install -g solc`

This uses npm to install the solc solidity compiler globally on your system.

2. Check it installed properly by running: `solcjs --version`

Now you can compile .sol Solidity files into EVM bytecode using the solc compiler.

Ganache

Ganache provides a personal Ethereum blockchain that runs locally on your machine for development and testing.

Think of Ganache as a simulated blockchain environment. It generates addresses with test ether you can use.

To install Ganache:

1. Go to https://www.trufflesuite.com/ganache and download the application for your OS.
2. Install and open the application. It will generate a personal test blockchain with dummy accounts and 100 ETH each.
3. You can customize settings like number of accounts and default balance.

Ganache gives you a personal sandbox blockchain to deploy and test contracts.

Metamask Browser Extension

Metamask is a crypto wallet browser extension that allows you to interact with the Ethereum blockchain.

Installing it on Chrome allows testing the wallet functionality with your local Ganache chain. Here's how to set it up:

1. Download Metamask from https://metamask.io/download.html on Chrome.

2. Create a wallet and save your seed phrase securely.
3. Connect Metamask to your Ganache blockchain by choosing Custom RPC and entering the RPC server details from Ganache.

Now you can use Metamask to transact on the Ganache testnet.

Truffle Suite

Truffle is a popular development framework for Ethereum smart contracts. It provides tools for compiling, testing, and deploying Solidity code.
To install Truffle:
1. Run `npm install -g truffle` in your terminal.
2. Initialize a new project by running `truffle init` in an empty project directory. This creates a skeleton Truffle project.
3. The key folders are:
   - Contracts - for Solidity contract code
   - Migrations - for deploy scripts
   - Test - for JS based contract tests
   - Truffle-config.js - for network configuration
4. Write contracts in the /contracts folder and tests in /test folder.
5. Use `truffle compile` and `truffle test` to build and test.

Truffle provides a robust framework for end-to-end smart contract development.

Step 2 - Design the Token

Before writing the smart contract code, you need to decide on the key parameters and design for your ERC-20 token.

Token Name and Symbol

The token name and symbol are ERC-20 metadata that identify your token.
For example, Chainlink's token name is "Chainlink" and symbol is "LINK".
Follow these best practices when deciding on a name/symbol:
- Keep the name short and easy to remember.
- Make sure the symbol is 3-5 characters max. This keeps fees lower.
- Check Etherscan to make sure your desired name/symbol are not already taken.
- Pick something that relates to your project concept and captures the utility.

Total Token Supply

The total supply determines how many tokens will ever exist. This is set permanently in the contract.
Some best practices for total supply:

- Pick a reasonable total that aligns to the token's purpose and your distribution plans. Billions can work for utility tokens, lower supplies for niche tokens.
- The supply must be set high enough that you have enough tokens to seed an active market.
- But avoid an extreme oversupply, which can make individual tokens appear worthless. Finding the right balance is key.
- Consider the impact on perception - higher supplies signal higher potential circulation, which can deter investors expecting scarcity.

Decimal Places

ERC-20 tokens have flexible decimal precision. Decimals allow dividing a token into smaller sub-units.

For example, 18 decimals means dividing 1 token into 10^{18} = 1,000,000,000,000,000,000 units. Guidelines for picking decimals:

- Utility tokens typically have 18 decimals for ample granularity.
- Coins used as currency may limit to 2-4 decimals for everyday convenience.
- More decimals also raise gas costs as precision multiplies.

Minting Process

Determine how new tokens will be created and added to circulation - aka minting. Common approaches:

- Mint all tokens upfront to the creator account.
- Stage minting over time, especially for multi-round sales.
- Mint based on activity, like rewarding users.
- Hybrid - mint initial supply and mint more later based on specific criteria.
- Ensure minting logic aligns to your distribution model and promotes fair supply growth.

Token Distribution

You need a model for how tokens will be distributed initially and over time. Typical distribution methods:

- Presale reserved for whitelisted buyers
- Public token sale
- Founder's endowment
- Community rewards
- Fundraising reserves
- Network incentives like staking rewards

Plan percentages for each distribution pool depending on your goals. Document it in a public token distribution schedule.

Token Utility

Issue tokens with a clear utility and value proposition beyond speculation. Possibilities include:

- Payment for services
- Discounted platform access
- Governance voting rights
- Staking and rewards
- Representing real world or digital assets

Outline concrete scenarios where people need the token and its benefits.

Step 3 - Write the Smart Contract

Now we can start coding the smart contract that will implement the ERC-20 token's functionality:

Import Libraries

In Solidity, you can import existing code libraries using:

solidity
Copy code

```
import "<LibraryName>"
```

For ERC-20 tokens, import these OpenZeppelin contracts:

```
import "@openzeppelin/contracts/token/ERC20/ERC20.sol"; import "@openzeppelin/contracts/access/Ownable.sol";
```

This gives you access to secure, audited implementations of ERC-20 logic and basic contract ownership.

Contract Definition

Define your contract name, make it inherit ERC20, Ownable, and set a constructor:

solidity
Copy code

```
contract MyToken is ERC20, Ownable { constructor()
ERC20("MyToken", "MTK") { // constructor logic } }
```

This sets up the basic contract structure.

Variables

Declare variables needed like total supply and the owner address:
solidity
Copy code

```solidity
uint256 public constant TOTAL_SUPPLY = 1000000 * (10**18);
address public owner;
```

Use appropriate data types like uint, address, string, etc.

Mappings

Define mappings to store balances, allowances, and other token data:
solidity
Copy code

```solidity
mapping(address => uint256) private _balances; mapping(address
=> mapping(address => uint256)) private _allowances;
```

Mappings act like hash tables to efficiently store token state.

Functions

Write key ERC-20 functions like transfer, transferFrom, approve, etc. Use the ERC20 inheritances to save time:
solidity
Copy code

```solidity
function transfer(address to, uint256 amount) public override
returns (bool) { _transfer(msg.sender, to, amount); return true;
}
```

Follow the ERC-20 interface spec for required functions.

Events

Log events for transfers, approvals, etc.
solidity
Copy code

```
event Transfer(address indexed from, address indexed to, uint256
value)
```

This creates a public record of transactions.

Modifiers

Use modifiers like onlyOwner to restrict access:
solidity
Copy code

```
modifier onlyOwner() { require(msg.sender == owner); _; }
```

This locks functions to the contract owner.

Constructor

The constructor runs on deployment to initialize state:
solidity
Copy code

```
constructor() { _mint(msg.sender, TOTAL_SUPPLY); owner =
msg.sender; }
```

Often used to mint initial tokens.
This covers the key steps in coding an ERC-20 token contract.

Step 4 - Test the Smart Contract

Once your ERC-20 token contract code is written, it needs thorough testing before deployment.
Here are tips for testing using Truffle:

Test Environment

Ensure Ganache is running to provide a local test blockchain.

Compile the contracts in Truffle first.

Copy code

```
truffle compile
```

This builds the contract artifacts needed for testing.

Deployment Script

In the /migrations folder, create a deployment script.
For example:

js
Copy code

```js
const MyToken = artifacts.require("MyToken"); module.exports = function (deployer) { deployer.deploy(MyToken); };
```

This handles deploying the contract.

Sample Tests

In the /test folder create JavaScript test files like:

js
Copy code

```js
const MyToken = artifacts.require("MyToken");
contract("MyToken", accounts => { it("should set the total supply on deployment", async () => { const myTokenInstance = await MyToken.deployed(); const totalSupply = await myTokenInstance.totalSupply();
assert.equal(totalSupply.toNumber(), 1000000); }); });
```

This checks the total supply after deploying.
You need many tests to cover each core function.

Running Tests

In the terminal, run:

Copy code

```
truffle test
```

This executes all the test cases and provides pass/fail results.
Your goal is 100% code coverage with passing tests.

Debugging

Use console.log statements to output values and debug errors:

js
Copy code

```
console.log("Token balance: " + balance)
```

Review failed test cases and debug errors until all tests pass.
Thorough unit testing is essential before launching your ERC-20 token to catch any issues.

Step 5 - Deploy to a Testnet

After thoroughly testing your ERC-20 token contract locally, it's time to deploy it on a public
Ethereum testnet before mainnet.

Choose a Testnet

Popular Ethereum testnets include Ropsten and Rinkeby.
Ropsten is ideal for initial testing as it mimics the main network closely.

Faucets

You need test ETH to deploy and transact on testnets.
Use faucets like Ropsten Ethereum Faucet to get ETH based on social actions.
Save and manage testnet ETH just like real ETH.

Configure Truffle

In truffle-config.js, define the testnet networks:

```js
Copy code
ropsten: { provider: () => new HDWalletProvider(), network_id:
3, }
```

This points Truffle to Ropsten.

Deploy

Run this to deploy to Ropsten:
```
Copy code
truffle migrate --network ropsten
```

It will deploy using your test ETH balance.

Verify on Etherscan

Go to Etherscan's Ropsten Explorer.
Search for your contract address and verify it.
This publishes your contract's source code publicly on the testnet.

Transact

Use Metamask pointed to Ropsten to transact with your deployed contract.
Send test tokens between accounts and ensure correct balances.
This confirms everything works end-to-end.

Rinkeby Repeat

Repeat the deployment on Rinkeby for further testing.
Use Rinkeby's Explorer to verify and inspect transactions.
Testing across multiple testnets increases confidence before mainnet.

Step 6 - Plan the Token Sale

Once your ERC-20 token contract is deployed and tested, it's time to plan how you will distribute
tokens through a sale event.

Sale Model

There are several formats you can choose from for your token sale:
- Presale - Token reserved for private early buyers before public sale
- Public Sale - Fixed price and open participation
- Dutch Auction - Declining token price over sale period
- Interactive Coin Offering - Buyers set the price through bids
- Launchpad - Sale through a platform like Polkastarter or TrustSwap
- Liquidity Bootstrapping - Price starts high and declines based on demand

Evaluate pros, cons, and your goals to pick the optimal model.

Pricing and Valuation

Determine your token's initial price and how many tokens represent ownership percentage:
- Price can be set or dynamic based on the sale model
- Consider comparator valuations of similar projects when setting percentage ownership per token
- Factor in potential appreciation - discount initial price to incentivize early buyers

Caps and Constraints

Set parameters like:
- Hard cap - maximum amount to raise in USD or ETH
- Individual contribution caps - limit whale purchases
- Minimum contribution - set buy-in floor
- Lockup periods - restrict sale of founder tokens

This ensures fair distribution and prevents manipulation.

Distribution Splits

Allocate percentages of the total supply across:
- Token sale portion
- Founders and development team
- Advisors and partners
- Community rewards
- Reserve allocation

Document the percentages transparently so buyers understand the splits.

Marketing and Listing

Promote the sale through crypto forums, email lists, influencers, etc.
Plan exchange listings immediately after launch to build momentum.

Step 7 - Launch the Token Sale

Once you've planned out your token sale model, pricing, and parameters, it's time to launch it and start distributing tokens.

Launch Website

Create a website dedicated to your new token. Include:
- Project overview and whitepaper
- Token sale details and timeline
- Token distribution splits
- Team bios
- Roadmap
- FAQ

This builds trust and awareness pre-launch.

Token Sale Portal

Integrate a web portal that allows buying tokens by sending ETH. Popular options:
- OpenZeppelin Tokensale Contract + Web3 Forms
- Coconut for managing KYC and payments
- ICO Wizard by TokenMarket

Guide buyers through identity verification, sale terms, ETH payment, and receipt of tokens.

Airdrop

Allocate a small portion of tokens to early supporters.
This helps create community awareness before public sale.

Marketing Push

Leverage social media, PR, influencers, ads, email lists to drive interest in your sale.
Time major announcements to maintain momentum.

Launch!

Start the countdown timer and allow public ETH contributions according to your sale parameters.
Track participation and tap into your marketing channels to promote in real-time.
Upon hitting your cap, close the sale and finalize accounting. Then distribute the tokens.

Step 8 - Distribute Tokens and List on Exchanges

Once your token sale concludes, the final step is distributing tokens and getting them trading publicly:

Token Distribution

Based on the sale participation data:
- Mint and transfer tokens to contributors' Ethereum addresses
- Programmatically distribute any vested founder, team, advisor, etc tokens
- Send community airdrop tokens
- Allocate any platform or ecosystem reserve

Accurately follow the published distribution percentages.

Liquidity and Listing

Add token liquidity to DEX exchanges like Uniswap and PancakeSwap.
Submit applications to get listed on centralized exchanges like Binance, Coinbase, and Kraken.
List on aggregators like CoinMarketCap, CoinGecko, Blockfolio to increase visibility.
Having buyers see tokens in their wallet and trading helps establish legitimacy.

Staking and Governance

Launch staking rewards and governance features if applicable.
This incentivizes holding tokens and builds community.

Continued Development

Keep token utility and adoption momentum going by launching your intended DApp, game, platform that leverages the token.
Consistently hitting technology roadmap milestones maintains confidence.

Chapter 9: Advanced Tokenomics and Distribution Strategies

While the previous chapters covered the technical build of an ERC-20 token, distributing and structuring the token supply properly is equally important. This chapter explores key concepts in tokenomics - the economics underpinning crypto tokens.

Token Distribution Models

There are various models to distribute tokens initially:

- Pre-mines - The developers mint all tokens upfront. This provides certainty but less community involvement.
- Fair launches - No pre-mine. Tokens are publicly minted over time through mining or other participation.
- Founder vesting - Locking up founder/team tokens for a period of time to show commitment.
- Community/Air drops - Offering a portion of supply for free to kickstart engagement.
- Token sales - Selling tokens in batches over multiple rounds of fundraising.

Each model aligns to different goals. Combinations can be used as well.

Managing Liquidity

Without adequate liquidity, markets for the token cannot emerge. Solutions include:

- Exchange listings - Getting added to centralized exchanges like Binance provides liquidity on day one.
- DEX incentives - Yield farming rewards for token pairs on Uniswap/PancakeSwap seeded by the team.
- Market making - Hiring traders to provide buy and sell orders in the early days.
- Locked reserves - Committing a portion of supply to liquidity pools over time ensures depth.

Controlling Vesting and Releases

Vesting restricts transferability of tokens to ensure orderly circulation:

- Founder/team vesting - 1-4 year graduated unlocking of tokens as a commitment mechanism.
- Advisor vesting - Unlocking advisor tokens based on milestones achieved.
- Investor vesting - Locking up investor/VC tokens post-sale for a fixed duration.
- Community vesting - Releasing tokens that encourage participation and engagement over time.

Modeling Metadata Fully

Metadata like capped supply and vesting parameters should be encoded in the token contract to provide clarity to buyers.

Chapter 10: ERC-20 Token Types and Use Cases

While basic fungible ERC-20 tokens are a common starting point, there are many token substandards tailored for specific utility. This chapter surveys some advanced token types.

Payment Tokens

Tokens intended as currencies on their blockchain. Examples are ETH on Ethereum or BNB on Binance Smart Chain. Features include:

- Capped supply with monetary policy like Bitcoin.
- Fast, low-cost transactions suitable for payments.
- Staking mechanisms that promote holding long-term.
- Strong liquidity and payment integrations.
- Minimal vesting to encourage usage as currency.

Securities Tokens

Tokens that represent ownership of real-world assets like equity, debt, or physical property. For example:

- Equity-based tokens can pay dividends.
- Asset-backed tokens directly linked to gold/oil reserves.
- Real estate tokens that distribute rental income.
- Strict regulatory compliance for investor protection.

Reward and Reputation Tokens

Used to incentivize actions that benefit a network or community. For example:

- Reward tokens distributed for contributions, like writing content or developing open source code.
- Reputation tokens allocating governance voting power based on community standing.
- Loyalty tokens that provide discounts or perks based on activity or holdings.
- Referral tokens for promoting a product or service.

There are endless possibilities to craft tokens tailored to a specific utility. Combinations of token features can be used as well. Developing a novel token type or use case is a key way projects can differentiate themselves in a crowded ecosystem.

Chapter 11: Alternative Blockchains Supporting Ethereum Smart Contracts

While Ethereum is the most proven blockchain for launching ERC-20 tokens, there are now several additional "Ethereum Virtual Machine" (EVM) compatible networks gaining adoption. This chapter explores the tradeoffs between Ethereum and new alternative chains.

Polygon (formerly MATIC)

- Ethereum sidechain using Plasma bridges back to mainnet Ethereum.
- Much faster and cheaper transactions than Ethereum.
- Wide range of DeFi and dApps deployed on Polygon.
- Simpler mainnet integration compared to standalone chains.
- Less decentralized and secure than Ethereum mainnet currently.

Binance Smart Chain (BSC)

- EVM-compatible blockchain built by Binance exchange.
- Very fast and extremely low transaction fees.
- Centralized validation through Binance node network.
- Numerous projects launching on BSC recently.
- Concerns over centralization and relationship to Binance.

Optimistic Ethereum

- "Optimistic rollups" compress transactions off-chain and post to Ethereum.
- Faster and lower fees than mainnet transactions directly.
- Inherits full security of Ethereum mainchain validation.
- Emerging technology, not fully decentralized yet.
- Interoperability enabled between Optimistic and mainnet.

There is no definitive choice - each network carries different advantages and risks profile. Assessing your priorities for speed, fees, security, and community support will determine the ideal environment to deploy your ERC-20 token.

Chapter 12: Leveraging Decentralized Exchanges

Decentralized exchanges (DEXs) like Uniswap have become popular ways to provide liquidity and enable trading for crypto tokens. This chapter explores capitalizing on DEXs to boost your token's circulation and accessibility.

Adding Token Liquidity

You can seed an initial liquidity pool for your token by:

- Providing an equal value of your tokens and ETH to Uniswap.
- Adding token pairs like USDC-YOURTOKEN for stablecoin trading.
- Setting attractive mining incentive rewards to attract liquidity providers.
- Increasing pooled amounts over time as your community grows.

Facilitating Trades

Once sufficient liquidity is added, trades between your token and ETH/stablecoins become possible by:

- Allowing anyone to freely trade your token through automated pool exchanges.
- Using arbitrage bots to ensure consistent pricing between DEXs and centralized exchanges.

- Providing info like price charts, 24 hr volume, and other metadata to attract trades.
- Working with DEXs to get your token prominently displayed with trade incentives.

Yield Farming and Staking

You can incentivize providing liquidity for your token by:
- Offering yield farming reward rates for your liquidity pairs.
- Distributing additional governance/utility tokens to liquidity providers.
- Enabling single-asset staking of your token for rewards.

DEXs have proven invaluable both for bootstrapping initial liquidity and building long-term decentralized and transparent trading. Integrating at the start ensures your token gains traction and an active ecosystem of holders.

Chapter 13: Securing Tokens - Web3 Wallets and Best Practices

Once your token is launched, proper security measures must be taken by holders to protect their tokens. This chapter provides an overview of Web3 wallet options and tips to maximize security. Web3 Wallets

Popular options for holding crypto assets include:
- MetaMask - Browser extension wallet for Ethereum assets and dApps.
- WalletConnect - Connects web apps to mobile wallets like Trust Wallet.
- Coinbase Wallet - Manages assets across different blockchains.
- Argent - Smart contract based wallet with security features.
- Ledger - Hardware wallet for offline asset storage and transaction signing.

Security Best Practices

Token holders should follow guidelines like:
- Use a hardware wallet for large holdings, paper wallet for cold storage.
- Never share private keys or recovery phrases.
- Enable 2FA on accounts when possible.
- Watch for fake apps impersonating legitimate wallets.
- Keep computers and phones used for crypto secure and malware-free.
- Diversify across multiple wallets to limit exposure of funds.

Following robust security practices is vital given the irreversible nature of blockchain transactions. Diligence to protect your newfound crypto wealth is essential.

Chapter 14: Marketing and Promoting Your Token Project

Creating a technically sound token is only the first step. Building an engaged community and generating buzz is vital for gaining adoption. This chapter explores marketing strategies for blockchain projects.

Social Media Presence
Leverage platforms like Twitter, Telegram, Discord, and Reddit to share project updates, engage users, and build an audience. Pay to promote key posts.

Influencers andAmbassadors
Onboard crypto leaders, YouTube creators, and key personalities to get exposure to their followings. Compensate them in tokens or money.

Conference and Meetups
Attend virtual and in-person crypto/blockchain conferences to interface with media, investors, and potential partners.

Grassroots Forums
Actively participate in relevant subReddits, forums, Facebook groups, etc. Answer questions and offer insights.

Content Marketing
Create guides, blogs, videos, and other informative content to attract organic search traffic. Promote through SEO.

Email Marketing
Build email lists to control touchpoints with users. Send project updates, newsletters, special offers, etc.

Paid Advertising
Experiment with paid search, social media ads, retargeting ads, and other formats to reach broad new audiences.

The blockchain space is flooded with projects. Standing out requires relentless community building and creativity both online and offline. A sound technical foundation paired with nonstop promotion is the formula to succeed.

Chapter 15: Learning from Successful Token Launches

While the crypto market is always evolving, there are lessons to be learned from previous successful token projects. This chapter spotlights a few case studies and founder interviews.

Case Study: Ethereum
- Raised over $18M in their 2014 token sale, with large purchases from VC firms.
- Earlier participants received larger allocations, building early interest.
- Founders were pioneers in the space with strong technical reputations.
- Clear utility as a smart contract development platform.
- Strong focus on documentation, transparency, and continuous progress.

Interview: Founder of VeChain
- Launched dual VEN/VET token structure to balance usage and investment.
- Built initial hype in China then expanded globally. Complied with regulations.
- Focused first on proving blockchain supply chain use case before tokenization.
- Patiently grew B2B utility value, then added token layer on robust foundation.

Case Study: Chainlink
- Advisors like Ari Juels added credibility during 2017 ICO boom.
- Technical oracle problem they solved was deeply needed yet overlooked.
- Slow steady growth for years before exploding based on real utility.
- Founders put in the work rather than hungry for quick capital.

There are no shortcuts to building long-term token value. But learning best practices from veteran projects can help pave the smoother road to success.

Chapter 16: Launching Your Token - A Roadmap and Checklist

Careful planning and preparation is required to successfully get a new ERC-20 token operational. This robust roadmap template and checklist covers all the key stages:

6-8 Months Out

Research competition, viability, and value proposition
Select blockchain platform (Ethereum, BSC, etc)
Assemble core team and advisors
Create business plan, budget, and projections
Design token economics model
Develop corporate structure and governance plan
Create operational processes and policies
Design branding and marketing assets
Build community channels (social media, email lists)
Create content strategy and release timeline

Identify community partners and influencers

4-6 Months Out

finalize token model, distribution schedule, sale parameters
Model monetary policy and stability mechanisms
Create litepaper draft detailing token utility
Develop smart contract specifications
Audit smart contract code thoroughly
Create detailed token sale documentation
Setup payment and KYC/AML processes
Test transaction speed, gas costs
Evaluate exchange listing options
Establish vesting schedules

2-4 Months Out

Release public litepaper, business plan, docs
Launch marketing campaigns across channels
Airdrop tokens to key supporters
Begin social media advertising to build buzz
Finalize economic models and simulations
Complete third-party auditing of contracts, finances
Ensure legal and regulatory compliance
Start pre-sale and private investor outreach
Develop staking, governance, and incentive programs

1 Month Out

Announce public token sale date, terms
Launch dedicated token sale website
Implement KYC verification processes
Test transaction interfaces and wallets
Verify exchange listings and liquidity partners
Complete smart contract security analyses
Simulate sale events to predict gas, volume etc.
Recruit community moderators and support volunteers

Token Sale Period

Manage inbound questions, communications
Provide 24/7 technical support

Monitor transactions, gas, volume closely
Execute marketing and promotion in real-time
Film AMAs and development video updates
Celebrate reaching cap and closing the sale

Post Sale

Distribute tokens to contributors' wallets
Initiate exchange listings and liquidity pools
Launch staking rewards and governance portals
Continue marketing to build organic community
Analyze data and feedback to refine processes
Survey contributors and community for input
Plan next stages of roadmap and development

With extensive planning and preparation using a roadmap guide like this, your next ERC-20 token launch has the greatest chance of succeeding and gaining significant traction in this competitive market.

Chapter 17: Next Steps on Your Blockchain Journey

Congratulations, you now have all the foundational skills to successfully build, launch and manage your own ERC-20 token! This concluding chapter provides some recommendations on where to go from here to continue mastering blockchain development.

- Expand your Solidity skills by taking advanced courses, studying complex contract code, and building a variety of projects beyond just tokens.
- Dive deeper into decentralized finance by creating lending protocols, AMM exchanges, margin trading platforms, and more.
- Look into alternate blockchain platforms like Cardano, Solana, Polkadot, etc. and learn their programming languages.
- Implement more advanced token functionality like vesting schedules, minting logic, burning, flash loans, andCornixOS integration.
- Develop expertise in Web3 frontend development using React.js and help build out dApps.
- Branch into areas like NFTs, gaming, metaverses, DAOs, supply chaintracking, and more.
- Immerse yourself in blockchain communities, discuss ideas, and stay on top of the fast-moving trends in this space.

Here are some recommended resources for further learning:

- Ethereum.org Developer Portal
- Chainshot - Web3 Development Lessons
- CryptoZombies - Interactive Solidity Course
- BuildSpace - Web3 Project Bootcamp
- Reactiflux - Discord Community
- DappUniversity - YouTube Channel

The world of blockchain is a playground for boundless innovation. This book provided the launch pad - now keep challenging yourself to create something remarkable!

Launching Your Own Token - Popular Niches and Trends

You now have all the core knowledge needed to create and distribute your own ERC-20 token. As a final note, here are some of the hottest niches and trends to consider when brainstorming token ideas:

DeFi - Decentralized Finance

DeFi is disrupting traditional finance using blockchain. Potential token use cases include governance tokens, liquidity provider rewards, crypto lending platforms, synthetic assets, and more.

NFTs - Non-Fungible Tokens

The NFT explosion is just getting started. Tokens can represent ownership of digital art, music, videos, virtual land, exclusive content and much more.

Gaming

Crypto-powered gaming is driving new models like play-to-earn. In-game tokens and assets, betting tokens, virtual currencies, and governance tokens provide engaging utility.

Metaverse

Virtual world and metaverse platforms need tokens to power virtual economies. Tokens can enable purchasing digital goods, virtual land, avatar customizations, staking, and more.

Web3

The growth of Web3 fuels demand for tokens with utility in decentralized storage, decentralized computing, DAO governance, contributor rewards, and beyond.

Fan Communities

Loyal fan bases for influencers, artists, creators, thinkers, and brands present ready markets. Tokens allow fans to support and interact with what they love.

Niche Interests

Niche communities from tech to health to art enthusiasts can rally around shared passion points. A token adds incentives, governance, rewards, and funding.
These categories should spark ideas on how you can stand out with a unique token tailored to a specific industry, group, or emerging use case. Tap into your own interests and knowledge!
With this complete guide, you have all the pieces needed to successfully create, launch and distribute your own ERC-20 token on Ethereum. Now get out there, engage your community, and bring your token vision to life!